Keep kindness forever in your heart

Design by Jason Phinney. Typeset in Myriad Pro and Emily Jane font. The illustrations in this book were rendered in oil by Jessica Mattea Dupree. Cover art by Jessica Mattea Dupree. Cover design by Jason Phinney. Art digitally enhanced by Lenny Paws Press.

Text copyright 2019 by Jason Phinney. Illustrations copyright 2019 by Jessica Mattea Dupree. All rights Reserved. No part of this may be reproduced in any form without written permission from the publisher.

Paperback ISBN 978-1-7336141-7-7
Hardcover ISBN 978-0-9969428-9-8

Lenny Paws Press Williamsburg, Virginia
learn more at www.lennypawspress.com

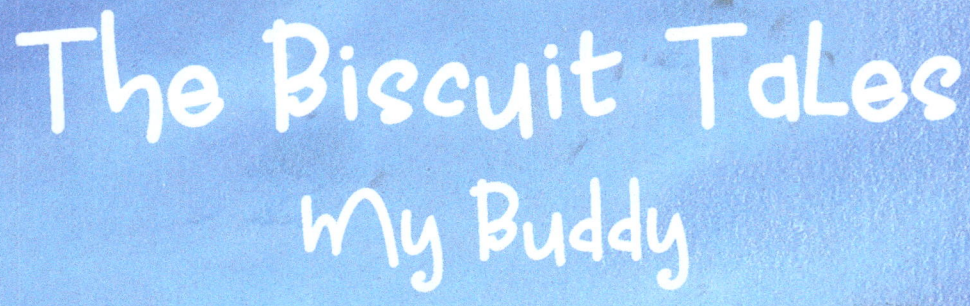

The Biscuit Tales
My Buddy

by Jason Phinney

illustrated by Jessica Mattea Dupree

I'm not certain who I am;
I wasn't called a name...
at least, not one I know of
by those from which I came

to wander down these lonely streets,
hoping to find some food.
Why they left me here alone,
I never understood.

Shivering, with soaking fur,
paws tired and in pain,
I snuck into a woodshed
to shelter from the rain.

I made a little mattress,
from mulch strewn on the floor,
and slept with one eye open
when he came through the door:

a large and fearsome canine,
with fur of brown and black.
If I didn't mind my manners,
he looked like he'd attack!

"Who said that you could sleep here?
I'd really like to know!
This is not the place for you;
you're gonna have to go!"

"Please kind sir, I'm begging you;
don't make me leave this farm!
Outside it's cold and rainy;
I won't cause any harm."

"You had better get on up
and get on down the lane.
If the owner finds you here,
we'll both be in the rain.

I work here as a guard dog
so I can't take a chance
and risk the food he throws me
when I go beg and dance."

I gathered up my courage
and headed for the door,
but there the big dog stopped me;
he'd thought of something more.

"I know I might regret it,
but what else can I do?
If you can keep real quiet,
I'll share my food with you."

He led me to an old barn,
past giant bales of hay,
then disappeared behind the wall,
returning soon to say,

"Have some of these biscuits here;
I saved them from last week."
I swallowed down three ones whole,
before I took a peek

and noticed he was watching
with tears welled in his eyes.
I asked what was the matter
that made the big dog cry.

He said that he had never seen
a skinny thing like me,
whose coat was dull and worn out
with ribs all plain to see.

"I'm gonna call you Biscuit;
you really wolfed those down!
The folks 'round here all know me;
they call me Buddy Brown."

He asked about my journey:
where I'd been and what I'd done.
I asked a million questions
and he answered every one.

"I think I'll keep you hidden
in the old horse barn out back.
If the owner gets too close,
the ducks will surely quack!"

Then Buddy introduced me to
his friend, Simone Raccoon,
and asked her to take care of me
so I'd feel better soon.

"Why yes, I'll help this little girl.
Although I must confess,
she looks so weak and skinny;
her coat is such a mess!

It's brittle and it's dirty;
in places it's not there.
I hope that I can salvage
a little of her hair!"

I'll wash and brush your tattered fur
to make it look real nice.
Dear, you need some weight on you;
we'll have to feed you twice!

Now sit right down; I'll fix you up;
your health will come along.
Each day will feel much brighter;
you'll sing a brand new song!"

My Buddy trained me daily;
he showed me all the ropes,
so I could be a partner
and help the pack to cope.

He taught me how to forage
through garbage cans at night
and how to find the rabbits
who always hid from sight.

Yet even with my efforts,
the times had gotten tough.
We shared the food we captured,
but never had enough.

Then one day, a car appeared,
and parked along the street.
A man got out, looked my way,
and left a tasty treat

for me, Simone, and Buddy,
to eat and get our fill.
We eagerly awaited
the long, cold hours 'til

he again returned at dawn,
delivering more food.
We filled up then ate some more;
it brightened up our mood!

Each morning, he arrived here
as weeks and weeks went by.
My body grew much stronger;
my spirit learned to fly!

The hunting trips were canceled;
the garbage raids were done.
No longer did we struggle;
the time had come for fun!

Bellies full, we ran and played;
chased ducks across the pond.
Happy times we shared each day
made stronger our deep bond.

I was so very lucky
my Buddy took me in.
I never would have made it
alone and cold and thin.

A little act of kindness
can sometimes be enough
to turn around another's life
when times have gotten tough.

My days are so much brighter
with my Buddy and Simone.
Because we're all together,
I will never feel alone.

Printed in the USA
CPSIA information can be obtained
at www.ICGtesting.com
LVHW071425101224
798790LV00011B/232